Saṃgharakkhita's

VUTTODAYA

A Study of Pāli Metre

Pali text & Translated into English by

R. SIDDHARATHA

Preface by

Prof. J. W. De Jong

Australian National University,
Canberra, Australia

SRI SATGURU PUBLICATIONS
INDIA

Published by :

Sri Satguru Publications,
First Floor,
40/5. Shakti Nagar,
Delhi-110007,
India.

First Edition : Calcutta 1929
Second Edition : Delhi 1981
Price : Rs. 50.

Printed in India.

Preface

Saṁgharakkhita, the author of the Vuttodaya, was a pupil of Sāriputta, according to G. P. Malalasekera (The Pali Literature of Ceylon, Colombo, 1928, p. 190) perhaps the brightest among the constellations that adorned Ceylon's literary firmament during the reign of Parākramabāhu (1153-1186). Saṁgharakkhita was a specialist in grammar, rhetoric and prosody, His Vuttodaya is the only extant Pāli work on prosody. It is based mainly upon Kedārabhaṭṭa's Vṛttaratnākara. He also quotes from Halāyudha's commentary on Piṅgala's Chandaḥsūtra.

The Vuttodaya has been very popular both in Burma and in Ceylon and several commentaries on it have been written by Burmese scholars, cf. Helmer Smith's Epilogomena to Volume I of the Critical Pāli Dictionary (Copenhagen, 1948), pp. 59–60. The Vuttodaya was first translated into English by Major G. E. Fryer: Pāli studies no. 2. The Pāli text of the Vuttodaya, or 'Exposition of metre', by Sangharakkhita Thera, with translation and notes, Journal of the Asiatic Society of Bengal, 46 (1877), 1, pp. 369-410. R. Siddharatha's edition and translation were published in the Journal of the Department of Letters, University of Calcutta, vol. 18 (1929), no. 7. Helmer Smith has explained the metrical terminology of the Vuttodaya in an appendix on Pāli metrics to his edition of Aggavaṁsa's Saddanīti, vol. IV (Lund, 1949), pp. 1148-1172. Recently the Vuttodaya has been translated into Japanese by Ichirō Katayama in Buddhist Studies (Bukkyō kenkyū). vol. 3 (August 1973), pp. 143-105, In his bibliography Katayama lists several Burmese and Singhalese editions of the Vuttodaya and its commentaries. His translation is based upon a recent Burmese edition (Buddhasāsana Press, 1968) and upon several commentaries, including a Singhalese commentary by Labugama Laṅkāna[illegible] (1946) and a Burmese commentary entitled Chandamedanī by Nandamañju (1970).

Siddhartha's edition and translation seem to have remained largely unknown and are not mentioned by Helmer Smith and Katayama. The present photomechanical reprint will undoubtedly be very welcome.

Canberra 23 February 1981. J. W. de Jong.

Preface

Saṅgharakkhita, the author of the Vuttodaya, was a pupil of Sāriputta, according to G. P. Malalasekera (The Pali Literature of Ceylon, Colombo, 1928, p. 189) perhaps the brightest among the constellations that adorned Ceylon's literary firmament during the reign of Parakkamabāhu I (1153-1186). Saṅgharakkhita was a specialist in grammar, rhetoric and prosody. His Vuttodaya is the only extant Pali work on prosody. It is based mainly upon Kedārabhaṭṭa's Vṛttaratnākara. He also quotes from Halāyudha's commentary on Piṅgala's Chandaḥsūtra.

The Vuttodaya has been very popular both in Burma and in Ceylon and several commentaries on it have been written by Burmese scholars, cf. Helmer Smith's Catalogue in Volume I of the Critical Pali Dictionary (Copenhagen, 1948), pp. 59*-60*. The Vuttodaya was first translated into English by Major G. E. Fryer, Pali studies no. 2. The Pali text of the Vuttodaya, or 'Exposition of metre' by Saṅgharakkhita Thera, with translation and notes, Journal of the Asiatic Society of Bengal 46 (1877), 1, pp. 369-410. [illegible] edition and translation were published in the Journal of the Department of Letters, University of Calcutta vol. 18 (1929), no. 2. Helmer Smith has explained the metrical terminology of the Vuttodaya in an appendix on Pali metres to his edition of Aggavaṃsa's Saddanīti, vol. IV (Lund, 1949) pp. 1145-1171. Recently the Vuttodaya has been translated into Japanese by Ichirō Kataoka in Buddhist Studies [illegible] vol. 2 (August 1973), pp. [illegible]. In his translation Kataoka has used several Burmese and Singhalese editions of the Vuttodaya and its commentaries. His translation is based upon [illegible] edition (Buddhasāsana Press 1908) and upon several commentaries, including a Singhalese commentary by [illegible] (1896) and a Burmese commentary entitled Chandasāratthavikāsinī (1909).

[illegible]

Canberra, [illegible] [illegible]

CONTENTS

Namo Buddhāya.

VUTTODAYA.

PAṬHAMO PARICCHEDO.

FIRST CHAPTER.

1. Namatthu janasantāna—tamasantānabhedino,
Dhammujjalantarucino—Munindodātarccino.

Obeisance to the Great Sage who, as the moon breaks the darkness with its rays, breaks the mass of ignorance with his brilliant Dharma.

2. Piṅgalācariyādīhi—chandaṁ yamuditaṁ purā,
Suddhamāgadhikānaṁ taṁ—na sādheti yaticchitaṁ.

The Chanda (or Prosody) compiled by Piṅgalācariya and others in olden times does not serve the purpose of those who know only Suddhamāgadhī.[1]

3. Tato Māgadhabhāsāya—mattāvaṇṇavibhedanaṁ,
Lakkhalakkhaṇasaṁyuttaṁ—pasannatthapadakkamaṁ.

4. Idaṁ Vuttodayaṁ nāma-lokiyacchandanissitaṁ,
Ārabhiissamahaṁdāni· tesaṁ sukhavibuddhiyā.

Therefore, to make it easy for them to understand (the Chanda) I shall begin in Māgadhabhāsā[1] this (book) named Vuttodaya which concerns only Lokiyacchanda (*i.e.*, popular Prosody as opposed to the Vedic Prosody, etc.), and which includes within it both Mattābheda and Vaṇṇabheda (*i.e.*, the methods of composing lines both according to Mattās and according to letters).

[1] Suddhamāgadhi or Māgadhi is another name for Pāli.

N.B.—(1) "Lokiyacchanda" means the Prosody that is used in general composition as distinguished from that which is used in the Vedas and in the Tipiṭaka Pāli.

(2) "Mattāvaṇṇavibhedanaṁ." This indicates that there are two kinds of Vuttas or metres, namely, Mattāvutta and Vaṇṇavutta. Of them Mattāvutta means those metres which depend on the number of Mattās,[1] and Vaṇṇavutta means those metres which are guided by the number of Vaṇṇas.[1]

(3) "Lakkhalakkhaṇasaṁyuttaṁ." We shall find afterwards that the verse which defines a particular metre is itself composed in the same metre. In other words, the same verse is the formula and example.

5. Sabbaglāmnādigalahu—bhyā majjhantagurū jasā,
Majjhantalā ratetaṭṭha—gaṇā go garu lo lahu.

The Garu[2] (*i.e*, the long vowel, or even the short vowel that precedes a conjunct consonant or a Niggahita) is called "Ga," and the Lahu[2] (*i.e.*, the short vowel) is called "La." There are then eight Gaṇas (or feet composed of these Gurus and Laghus), namely, those which consist wholly of 'Ga' and 'La' are known as 'Ma' and 'Na' respectively, those which have 'Ga' and 'La' at the beginning are known as 'Bha' and 'Ya' respectively, those which have Guru in the middle and at the end are known as 'Jha' and 'Sa' respectively, and those which have 'La' at the middle and at the end are known as 'Ra' and 'Ta' respectively.

N.B.—(1) Lahu (or Laghu) and Garu (or Guru) are not synonymous with Rassa and Dīgha. All the Laghus are Rassas but all the Rassas are not Laghus as the Rassas that are followed by a conjunct consonant or a Niggahita (*i.e.*, Anuswāra) are taken as Gurus.

(2) Gaṇa literally means a collection. It is used in this

[1] Mattā is the time that we take in pronouncing a short vowel, and Vaṇṇa means a letter.

[2] The terms Guru and Laghu are also used as Garu and Lahu in Pāli.

book technically to mean a collection of three letters. This is the biggest unit of measurement of a line in Vaṇṇavutta. This is similar to the word 'Foot' in English prosody. Here these Gaṇas are eight in number, namely, Magaṇa, Nagaṇa, Bhagaṇa, Yagaṇa, Jagaṇa, Sagaṇa, Ragaṇa and Tagaṇa. Among these, **Magaṇa has three Gurus, as ⌣ ⌣ ⌣; Nagaṇa has three Laghus, as - - -; Bhagaṇa has a Guru at the beginning** followed by two Laghus as ⌣ - -; Jagaṇa has a Guru in the middle with a Laghu on each side, as - ⌣ -; Sagaṇa has a Guru at the end preceded by two Laghus, as - - ⌣; Ragaṇa has a Laghu in the middle with a Guru on each side, as ⌣ - ⌣; and Tagaṇa has a Laghu at the end preceded by two Gurus, as ⌣ ⌣ -.

The following Sanskrit verse, if committed to memory, will be very useful in remembering the arrangement of the Laghus and Gurus in different Gaṇas :

Mastrigurustrilaghuśca nakāro,
Bhādiguruḥ punarādilaghuryaḥ,
Jo gurumadhyagato ra lamadhyaḥ,
Sontaguruḥ kathitontalaghustaḥ.

The terms 'Ma,' 'Na,' etc., are sometimes used with the word 'Gaṇa' such as Magaṇa, Nagaṇa, Bhagaṇa, etc. But mostly they are used by themselves as in "Mo mo go go Vijjummālā."

6. Bhajasā sabbagalahū—pañcime saṇṭhitā gaṇā,
Ariyādimhi viññeyyā—gaṇo idha catukkalo.

It should be known that only the following five Gaṇas, namely, Bha, Ja, Sa, Sabbaguru, and Sabbalahu, occur in Ariyā and such other metres. Here (*i.e.*, in Ariyā, etc.) a Gaṇa has only four Kalās (*i.e.*, Mattās).

N.B.—(1) Kalā is another name for Mattā. Now, Mattā is the time that we take in making one wink, and this is also the time taken in pronouncing a short vowel. Thus a short vowel or a Laghu has only one Mattā, and a long vowel or a Guru has two Mattās. Thus a Gaṇa in Ariyā may be of one of the following forms :—

⌣ - - ; - ⌣ - ; - - ⌣ ; ⌣ ⌣ ; - - - - .

(2) It is to be noted that the term Gaṇa has been used here to indicate the collection of four Mattās, and not three letters as above.

7. Saṁyogādī ca dīgho ca—niggahītaparo ca yo,
Guru vaṅko padanto vā—rassoñño mattiko luju.

The vowel which stands before a conjunct consonant, or that which is long, or that which is followed by a Niggahīta (*i.e.*, Anusvāra), is called Guru and it is indicated by a curved line. The vowel that stands at the end of a line is also sometimes taken as Guru. The short vowel which has only one Mattā is (known as) La (or Laghu) and it is represented by a straight line.

N.B.—In English prosody the accented vowel is generally indicated by a straight line and the unaccented one by a curved line. But here we find that a contrary method is adopted.

8. Pare pādādisaṁyoge—yo pubbo garuvakkharo,
Lahū sa kvaci viññeyyo—tadudāharaṇaṁ yathā.

The vowel that has become Garu by standing before a conjunct consonant which stands at the beginning of a line, is sometimes taken as Lahu. The following is an example of it :—

(This means that the short vowel that stands at the end of a line is sometimes regarded as a Laghu even if there be a conjunct consonant at the beginning of the next line.)

"9. Dassanarasānubhavane—nibaddhagedhā jinassayaṁ janatā,
Vimhayajananī saññata—kriyā nu kaṁ nānuranjayati."

Here, in the third line the short vowel 'a' of 't' of the word 'saññata' stands before the conjunct consonant 'kri' of the word "kriyā" in the following line. It should therefore, be taken as a Guru according to the instruction given in the verse No. 7. But it is taken here as a Laghu. Otherwise, the line which is of an Ariyā is not correct metrically (*vide* verse 1, Ch. 2).

10. Viññeyyā lokato Saññā—samudoturasādinaṁ,
Pādo ñeyyo catutthaṁso—padacchedo yatibbhave.

From the world (*i.e.*, from the popular usage) should be learned the numerical value attached to the words Samudda, Utu, Rasa, etc. A Pāda is one fourth part of a verse, and a Yati is the breaking of the pāda.

N.B.—(1) In Pāli and Sanskrit literature numbers are often indicated by some words of numerical significance. Thus, Canda indicates one, because there is only one Canda, *i.e.*, moon; Nayana indicates two as there are two Nayanas, *i.e.*, eyes. This method is known as Bhūtasaṅkhyāvidhi.

(2) The terms Pāda and Pada are used here synonymously. Both are meant to indicate a line in a verse. Verses are generally composed of four lines and each of these is called a Pāda.

(3) Yati is what is called 'Pause' or caesura in English prosody.

11. Samamaddhasamaṁ vutaṁ—visamaṁ cāparaṁ tathā,
Samā lakkhaṇato pādā—cattaro yassa taṁ samaṁ.

12. Yassantimena dutiyo—tatiyenādimo samo,
Tadaddhasamamaññantu-bhinnalakkhṇamādikaṃ.

The Vutta (*i.e.*, Vaṇṇavutta) is of three kinds, namely, Sama, Addhasama and Visama. If the four Pādas or lines of a Vutta are similar in form that Vutta is called Sama, *i.e.*, Regular. If the second Pāda of any Vutta is similar in form to the last, and the first to the third, it is called Addhasama, *i.e.*, Semi-Regular. The other Vutta in which the lines are not similar to one another is called Visama, *i.e.*, Irregular.

N. B.—Here the word "Vutta" refers to the Verse composed in a particular Vutta.

13. Pādamekakkharārabbha—yāva chabbīsatakkharaṁ,
Bhave pādehi taṁ chandaṁ—nānānāmoditaṁ tato;

14. Daṇḍakā Caṇḍavuṭṭhyādi—pādehi chahi tīhi tu,
Gāthāti ca paratthevaṃ—chandosaññā pakāsitā.

There are Chandas varying from the line containing one letter up to the line containing twenty-six letters known by different names; and then after that (*i.e.*, after the Chanda containing twenty-six letters) there are Daṇḍakas such as Caṇḍavuṭṭhi, etc. The verses with either six or three lines are known as Gāthās. The names of the Chandas are thus given in other works (*i.e.*, in Sanskrit Prosody).

N. B.—The names of the Chandas are not given in serial order in the Vuttodaya. They are given below in their Pāli and the corresponding Sanskrit forms along with the number of Vuttas (*i.e.*, Metres) which each of them contains:

Number of letters.	Name of the Chanda.		Number of Vuttas.
	Pāli	Sanskrit	
1	Vuttā	Uktā	2
2	Accuttā	Atyuktā	4
3	Majjhā	Madhyā	8
4	Patiṭṭhā	Pratiṣṭhā	16
5	Suppatiṭṭhā	Supratiṣṭhā	32
6	Gāyattī	Gāyatri	64
7	Uṇhi	Uṣniḥ	128
8	Anuṭṭhubha	Anuṣṭup	256
9	Brahati	Bṛihati	512
10	Panti	Paṅkti	1024
11	Tuṭṭhubha	Triṣṭup	2048
12	Jagatī	Jagati	4096
13	Atijagati	Atijagati	8192
14	Sakkarī	Sakvari	16384
15	Atisakkarī	Atisakvari	32768
16	Aṭṭhī	Aṣṭī	65536
17	Accaṭṭhī	Atyaṣṭī	131072
18	Dhiti	Dhṛti	262144
19	Atidhiti	Atidhṛti	524288
20	Kati	Kṛti	1048576
21	Pakati	Prakṛti	2097152
22	Ākati	Ākṛti	4194304
23	Vikati	Vikṛti	8388608
24	Saṅkati	Saṅkṛti	16777216
25	Atikati	Atikṛti	33554432
26	Ukkati	Utkṛti	67108864

15. Anantaroditaṃ caññа—metaṁ sāmañña nāmato,
Gāthā micceva niddiṭṭhā—munindavacane pana.

But in the Buddhist literature all of these (*i.e.*, the Vaṇṇavuttas given above) and also others (*i.e.*, Mattāvuttas such as Ariyā, etc., which will be given below) are known by the general name of Gāthā.

N. B.—Chanda and Vutta. Chanda determines the number of letters. Vutta determines the arrangement of Gurus and Laghus. In one Chanda there are many Vuttas. Vuttā, Acuttā, etc., are Chandas, and Tanumajjhā, Kumāralalita, etc., are Vuttas.

16. Visesanāmato kiñci—gahetvā sabbatocitaṁ,
Dassayissāmahaṁ tvettha—nāmānāvibhavissare.

Here I shall show in their special names some of those which are quite suitable (for general use, or for the use in Pāli literature), and these names will appear afterwards (in their appropriate places).

Iti Vuttodaye saññāparibhāsāniddeso nāma Paṭhamo paricchedo.

Here ends the first Chapter of Vuttodaya dealing with names and signs.

DUTIYO PARICCHEDO.

SECOND CHAPTER.

ARIYĀ JĀTAYO.

The Ariyā Group.

1. Chaṭṭhokhilalahu jo vā—gayutāññechaggaṇā na jo visame,
Ariyāyantaddhe lo—chaṭṭhonte go gaṇā chaññe.

In Ariyā the sixth (gaṇa) will be of all-Laghu or Ja (*i.e.*, Jagaṇa). There are six other Gaṇas with a Ga (*i.e.*, Garu). There will be no Ja in odd places. In the last half the sixth (Gaṇa) will be of only a single La (*i.e.*, Laghu) and at the end there will be a Ga. And there are six other Gaṇas.

Explanation.

Ariyā (Sk. āryā) is divided into two halves or rather into two parts. Each of these parts contains seven Gaṇas and a Guru, the Guru being always at the end. In the first part the sixth Gaṇa is of four Laghus or a Jagaṇa. And in the second part the sixth Gaṇa contains only a single Laghu. In odd places in both the parts there should be no Jagaṇa.

The stanza given above is itself an example of Ariyā. Its Gurulaghu table can be drawn up as follows:—

◡ ◡, - - - -, ◡ ◡, - - ◡, ◡ ◡, - ◡ -, ◡ - -, ◡;

- - ◡, ◡ ◡, ◡ ◡, ◡ ◡, ◡ ◡, -, ◡ ◡, ◡.

N. B.—In Ariyā a Gaṇa has only four Mattās. See **Stanza 6, Ch. I.**

2. **Paṭhamaddhe chaṭṭho ce—sabbalahetthādilahuni bhavati yati.**

Tapparakontepi sace—carimepi bhavati catutthonte.

In the first half of Ariyā if the sixth Gaṇa contains a Sabbalahugaṇa (*i.e.*, if the sixth Gaṇa is of four Laghus), the Yati (*i.e.*, the pause) will fall on the first Laghu of that Gaṇa. But if the sixth Gaṇa has a Sabbalahugaṇa following it (*i.e.*, if the seventh is a Sabbalahugaṇa) then the Yati will fall on the last letter (of the sixth Gaṇa).

Again, in the second half if the fourth Gaṇa has a Sabbalahugaṇa following it (*i.e.*, if the fifth is a Sabbalahugaṇa) the Yati will fall on the last of the fifth Gaṇa.

(On the strength of the particle " Api " occurring in the verse, there can be a pause in the first letter of the fifth Gaṇa and this is the pause recognised by the Sanskrit prosodists.)

E.g.,

- - ⏑, ⏑ ⏑, ⏑ ⏑, ⏑ - -, ⏑ ⏑, -' - - -', - - - -, ⏑;

⏑ - -, ⏑ ⏑, - - ⏑', - - ⏑, - - - -', , ⏑ ⏑, ⏑.

In the above table the places marked by (,) are the places of the pause.

3. Ariyāsāmaññaṁce—pubboditalakkhaṇaṁ bhave yassā,

Ādimamatha pādayugaṁ—yassātyaṁsehi sā Pathyā.

If any stanza has all the characteristics of an Ariyā given above, and in addition to that the first Pāda of each half ends in three Gaṇas it is called Pathyā.

E.g.,

- - ⏑, ⏑ ⏑, ⏑ ⏑, ⏑ ⏑, - - ⏑, - ⏑ -, ⏑ ⏑, ⏑;

⏑ - -, - - ⏑, - - ⏑, ⏑ ⏑, ⏑ ⏑, -, ⏑ ⏑, ⏑.

Here we find that the first parts of both the halves end in the third Gaṇa.

4. Yattha gaṇattayamullaṅghiyo—bhayatthādimo bhave vipulā.

If in a stanzà of Ariyā the first parts of both the halves end somewhere after three Gaṇas it is called Vipulā.

E.g.,

⏑ - -, ⏑ - - , ⏑ ⏑ , - ⏑ -, ⏑ ⏑ , - ⏑ -, ⏑ - -, ⏑ .

This is only one part of Vipulā. Here we find that the first portion of this part ends in the middle of the fourth Gaṇa and not at the end of the third Gaṇa as in Pathyā.

5. Gurumajjhago jakāro—catutthako dutiyako Capalā.

If the second and the fourth Gaṇa of each of the two halves of Ariyā is a Jagaṇa and stands between two Gurus, it is called Capalā.

- - ⏑ , - [2]⏑ -, ⏑ ⏑ , - [4]⏑ - , ⏑ - -, -, ⏑ - -, ⏑ .

Here the 2nd and the 4th Gaṇas are Jagaṇas and each of them stands between two Gurus.

6. Capalāgataṁ khilaṁ ce—dalādimaṁ lakkhaṇaṁ bhajati yassā,
Pathyālakkhaṇamaññaṁ—Mukhacapalā nāma sā bhavati.

If the first half of a stanza has all the characteristics of the Capalā and the other (*i.e.*, the second half) has the characteristics of the Pathyā, it is called Mukhacapalā.

E.g.,

- - ⏑ , - ⏑ -, ⏑ ⏑ , - ⏑ - , ⏑ ⏑ , - ⏑ - , - - ⏑ , ⏑ ;

⏑ ⏑ , ⏑ - -, ⏑ ⏑ , - - - -, ⏑ ⏑ , -, ⏑ - -, ⏑ .

Here we find that the first part has the characteristics of Capalā, and the second part those of Pathyā.

7. Pathyāya lakkhanaṁ ce—pathamaddhe lakkhaṇaṁ tu Capalāyā,
Dutiye daletha yassā—pakittitā sā Jaghana capalā.

In a stanza if the characteristics of Pathyā are to be found in the first half, and those of Capalā in the second half it is called Jaghanacapalā.

E.g.,

⌣⌣, - ⌣ -, ⌣⌣, - - ⌣, ⌣⌣, - ⌣ -, - - ⌣, ⌣.
(Pathyā).

- - ⌣, - ⌣ -, ⌣⌣, - ⌣-, ⌣⌣, -, - - - -, ⌣.
(Capalā).

Iti Ariyājātayo.

Here ends the Ariyā Group.

Gīti Jātayo.

The Gīti Group.

1. Sabbaṁ paṭhama dale yadi—lakkhaṇamariyāyamutta-mubhayesu,
Yassā dalesu yuttaṁ—vuttā sā Gīti vuttayatilalitā.

If all the characteristics of the first half of Ariyā are found in both the halves of a stanza along with the Yatis (*i.e.*, pauses) mentioned above, it is called Gīti.

E.g.,

⌣⌣, - - - -, ⌣ - -, ⌣ - -, - - ⌣, - ⌣ -, - - ⌣, ⌣;

⌣⌣, - ⌣ -, ⌣⌣, ⌣⌣, ⌣⌣, - ⌣ -, - - - -, ⌣.

Here both the lines are composed in the form of the first line of Ariyā.

2. Ariyāyaṁ dutiyaddhe—gaditākhilalakkhaṇaṁ yaṃ taṃ,
Bhavati dalesubhayesupi—yadi yassā sāyamupagīti.

If all the characteristics of the second half of the Ariyā are found in both the halves of a stanza it is called Upagīti.

E.g.,

- - ⏑⏑, ⏑⏑ - -, ⏑⏑ ⏑⏑, - - ⏑⏑, - - ⏑⏑, -, ⏑⏑ ⏑⏑, ⏑⏑;

- - - -, ⏑⏑ - -, ⏑⏑ - -, - - ⏑⏑, ⏑⏑ ⏑⏑, -, - - ⏑⏑, ⏑⏑.

Here both the lines bear the characteristics of the second line of Ariyā.

3. Ariyāyaddhadvitayaṁ—pubboditalakkaṇūpetaṁ ;
Vipariyayenābhihitaṁ—yassā sambhavati ceha Upagīti.

If in a stanza the two halves of Ariyā of the above given characteristics are placed inversely it is called Upagīti.

E.g.,

- - ⏑⏑, ⏑⏑ ⏑⏑, - - ⏑⏑, ⏑⏑ ⏑⏑, - - ⏑⏑, -, ⏑⏑ ⏑⏑, ⏑⏑;

- - - -, ⏑⏑ ⏑⏑, - - ⏑⏑, ⏑⏑ ⏑⏑, ⏑⏑ - -, - ⏑⏑ -, - - ⏑⏑, ⏑⏑.

Here we find that the first line of the Ariyā is the second line in this stanza, and the second line of the Ariyā is the first line here.

4. Ariyāpubbaddhaṁ yadi-gurunekenādhikena nidhane yuttaṁ,
Yadi pubbaddhasamānaṁ—dalamitaraṁcoditāyamariyāgīti.

If the first part of the Ariyā gets one more Guru at the end (and stands as the first line of stanza), and the second line is just like the line so made, in other words, if the first part of Ariyā with an additional Guru at the end stands in both the lines of a stanza) it is called Ariyāgīti.

E.g.,

- - ⌣ , ⌣ ⌣ , ⌣ - - , - - ⌣ , ⌣ ⌣ , - ⌣ - , - - ⌣ , ⌣ , ⌣ ;

- - ⌣ , ⌣ - - , ⌣ ⌣ , - - - - , ⌣ ⌣ , - ⌣ - , - - ⌣ , ⌣ , ⌣ .

Here, but for the additional Guru, each of the two lines are just like the first line of Ariyā.

Iti Gītijatayo.

Thus ends the Gīti Group.

Vetālī Jātayo.

The Vetālī Group.

1. Visame cha siyuṁ kalā mukhe-sametaṭṭha ralagā tatopari,
Vetālīyaṁ tamuccate—lahuchakkaṁ na nirantaraṁ same.

If in a verse in the odd lines (*i.e.*, in the first and third lines) there are six Mattās at the beginning, and in the even lines (*i.e.*, in the second and the fourth lines) there are eight Mattās at the beginning, and both are followed by a Ragaṇa and a Laghu and a Guru, it is called Vetāliya. Here in the even lines there should not be six Laghus consecutively (Sk. Vaitālīya).

E.g.,

6 R. L. G. 8 R. L. G.

- - ⌣ - - , ⌣ - ⌣ , - ⌣ ⌣ ⌣ - - - , ⌣ - ⌣ , - , ⌣ ;

6 R. L. G. 8 R. L. G..

⌣ ⌣ ⌣ , ⌣ - ⌣ , - , ⌣ ; - - ⌣ ⌣ - - , ⌣ - ⌣ , - , ⌣ .

N.B.—(1) **Here the stanza is broken into four lines.**

(2) The **Vṛttaratnākara lays down that these Laghus should not** be made into Gurus by **mixing a Laghu** of an odd place **with a Laghu of a preceding even place.** But the Laghu of an odd place can be **mixed with a** Laghu of the following even place and made into a Guru. **For instance, the first and second Laghus can be made into a** Guru, but the second and the third cannot be.

2. Vetālīyopamaṁ mukhe taṁ—Opacchandasikaṁ rayāyadante.

In a verse if the **beginning** of the lines is like that in **Vetālīya,** but at the end there be a **Ragaṇa and a Yagaṇa** (instead of a Ragaṇa, a Laghu and a Guru) it is called Opacchandasika (Sk. Aupacchandasika).

E.g.,

6 R Y 8 R Y

⏑⏑⏑, ⏑-⏑, -⏑⏑, ⏑⏑⏑--, ⏑-⏑, -⏑⏑.

3. Āpātalikā kathiteyaṁ—bhaggānte yadi pubbamivaññaṁ.

If in a verse the beginnings of the lines are as given above, but at the end there are a Bhagaṇa and two Gurus it is called Āpātalikā.

E.g.,

6 Bha. G G 8 Bha. G G

⏑⏑--, ⏑--, ⏑, ⏑; ⏑⏑⏑--, ⏑--, ⏑, ⏑.

4. Yadādito Dakkhiṇantika—Thitetthapādesākhilesu jo.

If there be a Jagaṇa at the beginning of each line that kind of Vetālīya is called Dakkhiṇantikā (Sk. Dakṣiṇāntikā).

N.B.—This is only another form of Vetālīya where the first six Mattās are arranged so as to form a Jagaṇa, at the beginning.

E.g.,

J R L G J R L G

. ⏑ - ⏑ , ⏑ - ⏑ , - , ⏑ ; - ⏑ - ⏑ ⏑ , ⏑ - ⏑ , - , ⏑ .

6 8

5. Udiccavuttīti vuccate—jo cādo visamesu sanṭhito.

If the Jagaṇa stands at the beginning of the odd lines only that kind of Vetālīya is called Udiccavutti (Sk. Udīcyavṛtti).

E.g.,

J R L G 8 R L G

- ⏑ - ⏑ , ⏑ - ⏑ , - , ⏑ ; ⏑ ⏑ ⏑ - - , ⏑ - ⏑ , - , ⏑ .

6

6. Pubbattha samesu ce gajā—Paccavuttiruditeti sanṭhitā

If in the even lines there are a Guru and a Jagaṇa at the beginning that Vetālīya is called Paccavutti (Sk. Prācya-vṛtti).

E.g.,

6 R L G J R L G

⏑ ⏑ - - , ⏑ - ⏑ , - , ⏑ , ⏑ , - ⏑ - , - - , ⏑ - ⏑ , - , ⏑

7. Samāsamātrādinaṁ samā—saṁyutā bhavati taṁ Pavattakaṁ.

If the even and the odd lines of the above two, *i.e.*, Paccavutti and Udiccavutti, are respectively made the even and the odd lines of a verse it is called Pavattaka (Sk. Pravṛttaka).

E.g.,

Udiccavutti Paccavutti

- ⏑ - ⏑, ⏑ - ⏑, -, ⏑. ⏑, - ⏑ -, - -, ⏑ - ⏑, -, ⏑.

Here we find that the first part is similar to Udiccavutti and the second part to Paccavutti. Pavattaka is thus a mixture of Udiccavutti and Paccavutti.

N.B.—From Opacchandasika up to the Paccavutti the lines given must be doubled to make a complete verse.

8. Assa yā samakatā' parantikā.

A verse made of the even lines of this (Pavattaka) is called Aparantikā.

This means that if in a verse each of the four lines is similar to one of the even lines of Pavattaka (and hence also of Paccavutti) it is called Aparantikā (Sk. Aparāntikā).

E.g.,

⏑, - ⏑ -, - -; ⏑ - ⏑, -, ⏑;
⏑, - ⏑ -, - -; ⏑ - ⏑, -, ⏑;
⏑, - ⏑ -, - -; ⏑ - ⏑, -, ⏑;
⏑, - ⏑ -, - -; ⏑ - ⏑, -, ⏑.

9. Tadaññajā Cārubhāsinī.

If a verse is composed of lines other than the even lines (of Pavattaka) it is called Cārubhāsinī.

This means that if in a verse each of the four lines is similar to one of the odd lines of Pavattaka (and hence of Udiccavutti) it is called Cārubhāsinī.

E.g.,

- ⏑ - ⏑, ⏑ - ⏑, -, ⏑.
- ⏑ - ⏑, ⏑ - ⏑, -, ⏑.
- ⏑ - ⏑, ⏑ - ⏑, -, ⏑.
- ⏑ - ⏑, ⏑ - ⏑, -, ⏑.

Iti Vetālījātayo.

Thus ends the Vetāli Group.

Atha Mattāsamaka Jātayo.

The Mattāsamaka Group.

1. Dvikavihatavasulahuracaladhitiriha.

The verse that has in each of its lines eight Laghus multiplied by two (*i.e.*, sixteen Laghus) is called Acaladhiti (Sk. Acaladṛti).

E.g.,

- - - - - - - - - - - - - - - - .

- - - - - - - - - - - - - - - - .

- - - - - - - - - - - - - - - - .

- - - - - - - - - - - - - - - - .

N.B.—It is to be noted here that in this group of verses each line contains sixteen Mattās.

2. Mattāsamakaṁ navamolgante.

The verse that has in each of its lines a Laghu in the ninth place and a Guru at the end is called Mattāsamaka (Sk. Mātrāsamaka).

E.g.,

9 G

⌣ ⌣ - - ⌣ - - ⌣ ⌣ ⌣ .

N.B.—It is to be noted that in all the following lines there will be a Guru at the end.

3. Jonlāthavāṇṇavā Visiloko.

If in a line there is a Jagaṇa or a Nagaṇa along with a Laghu (*i.e.*, four Laghus) after four Mattās it is called Visiloka (Sk. Viśloka).

E.g.,

J

⏑ ⏑ , - ⏑ - , ⏑ - - ⏑ ⏑ . (Or a similar form).

If a Nagaṇa along with a Laghu is put instead of the Jagaṇa the line stands as follows :

N.L.

⏑ ⏑ , - - - - , ⏑ - - ⏑ ⏑ . (Or in some similar form).

4. Tadvayato Vānavāsikākhyā.

If there is a Jagaṇa or a Nagaṇa followed by a Laghu after eight Mattās it is called Vānavāsikā.

E.g.,

J

⏑ - - ⏑ ⏑ , - ⏑ - , ⏑ ⏑ .

Here in the place of the Jagaṇa we can insert a Nagaṇa and a Laghu.

E.g.,

⏑ - - ⏑ ⏑ , - - - - , ⏑ ⏑ .

5. Pañcaṭṭhanavasu yadi lo Citrā[1]

If there is a Laghu in the fifth, and eighth and ninth places the metre is called Citrā.[1]

E.g.,

⏑ ⏑ , - , - - , - , - , - ⏑ ⏑ ⏑ .

[1] Cittā in some editions.

6. Gallāṭṭhahi ce sā Upacitrā.[1]

If after eight Mattās there be one Guru and two Laghus (*i.e.*, a Bhagaṇa) the metre is called Upacitrā.[1]

E.g.,

⌣ ⌣ - - ⌣ , ⌣ - - , ⌣ ⌣ .

7. Yamatītalakkhaṇavisesayuta—Mattāsamādipādā b h i-hitaṁ,
Aniyatavuttaparimāṇasahitaṁ—pathitaṁ janesu Pādā-kulakaṁ.

The verse that is composed of the lines of Mattāsama and other metres (combinedly), with their abovementioned characteristics, but has no regularity of Vuttas in its lines is popularly called Pādākulaka.

E.g.,

- - ⌣ - ⌣ - - - ⌣ - - ⌣ ,
⌣ ⌣ - ⌣ - ⌣ ⌣ - - ⌣ ,
- - - - ⌣ - - - ⌣ - - - ⌣ ,
- - ⌣ - ⌣ - ⌣ ⌣ - - ⌣ .

Now, here the first line is Mattāsamaka as it contains a Laghu in the ninth place and a Guru at the end; or it may be a Visiloka as it has a Jagaṇa after four Mattās; or it may be Citrā as it has a Laghu in the fifth, eighth and ninth places. The second line is Visiloka. The third line is either Mattāsamaka or Vānavāsika. The fourth line is, again, Visiloka. Thus, in this stanza all the various metres mentioned above are mixed and therefore it is a Pādākulaka.

Iti Mattāsamaka Jātayo.

Thus ends the Mattāsamaka Group.

[1] Upacittā in some editions.

Vinā vaṇṇehi mattā gā,
Vinā vaṇṇā gurūhi tu,
Vinā lahūni guravo,
Dale Pathyādino matā.

In Pathyā and other metres (of its kind) the number of Mattās minus the number of letters is equal to the number of Gurus in the verse. Similarly, the number of Mattās minus the number of Gurus is equal to the number of letters. Again, the number of Mattās minus the number of Laghus divided by two is equal to the number of Gurus.

This computation can be set in the following tabular form :—

	No. of Mattās			− No. of Letters	=	No.	of Gurus.
	,,	,,	,,	− ,, ,, Gurus	=	,,	,, Letters.
½	(,,	,,	,,	− ,, ,, Laghus)	=	,,	,, Gurus.

E.g.,

In the above given Pathyā (see verse 3, Ch. 2) there are 57 Mattās, and 35 letters. Then the number of Gurus in it, according to the above computation, is 22. Similarly the number of letters, etc., can be found out.

Iti Mattāvuttaniddeso Nāma Dutiyo Paricchedo.

Thus ends the second Chapter dealing with Mattāvutta.

TATIYO PARICCHEDO.

THIRD CHAPTER.

Gāyatti (6 letters).

1. Tyā ce Tanumajjhā.

If (in each of the four lines of a verse) there is a Tagaṇa along with a Yagaṇa, the metre is called Tanumajjhā (Sk. Tanumadhyā).

E.g.,

⏑ ⏑ - / - ⏑ ⏑ .

N.B.—The Chandas of one, two, three, four and five letters are omitted here apparently because no verses are generally composed in them.

Uṇhi (7 letters).

2. Kumāralalitā jsgā.

(The metre which has) a Jagaṇa, Sagaṇa and a Guru, is called Kumāralalitā.

E.g.,

- ⏑ - / - - ⏑ / ⏑ .

Anuṭṭhubha (8 letters).

3. Citrapadā yadi Bhā gā.

If there are two Bhagaṇas and two Gurus, the metre is called Citrapadā.

E.g.,

⌣ - -/⌣ - -/⌣/⌣ .

4. Mo mo go go vijjummālā.

If there are two Magaṇas and two Gurus, the metre is called Vijjummālā (Sk. Vidyunmālā).

E.g.,

⌣ ⌣ ⌣ / ⌣ ⌣ ⌣ / ⌣ / ⌣ .

5. Bhā talagā Mānavakaṁ.

If after a Bhagaṇa there stand a Tagaṇa, a Laghu and a Guru, the metre is called Mānavakaṁ.

E.g.,

⌣ – – / ⌣ ⌣ – / – / ⌣.

6. Glā Samānikā rajā ca.

If there are a Guru and a Laghu and also a Ragaṇa and a Jagaṇa it is called Samānikā.

E.g.,

⌣ / – / ⌣ – ⌣ / – ⌣ – ,

7. Pamānikā jarā lagā.

The metre which has a Jagaṇa and a Ragaṇa and also a Laghu and a Guru is called Pamāṇikā (Sk. Pramāṇikā).

E.g.,

– ⌣ – / ⌣ – ⌣ / – / ⌣ .

N.B.—This is the converse of the above. Such things are not infrequent.

Brahati (9 letters).

8. **Rā nasā yadi Halamukhī.**

If after a Ragaṇa there stand a Nagaṇa and a Sagaṇa, the metre is called Halamukhī.

E.g.,

⏑ — ⏑ / — — — / — — ⏑

9. Bhujagasusubhatā nā mo.

If there are two Nagaṇas and a Magaṇa, the metre is called Bhujagasusubhatā (Sk. Bhujagaśiśubhṛtā).

E.g.,

— — — / — — — / ⏑ ⏑ ⏑ .

Panti (10 letters).

10. Msā jgā Suddhavirāditaṁ mataṁ.

The metre which has a Magaṇa, a Sagaṇa, a Jagaṇa, and a Guru, is called Suddhavirādita (Sk. Suddhavirad).

E.g.,

⏑ ⏑ ⏑ / — — ⏑ / — ⏑ — / ⏑

11. Mnā yo go yadi Paṇavo khyāto.

The metre which has a Magaṇa, a Nagaṇa, a Yagaṇa and a Guru is called Paṇava.

E.g.,

⏑ ⏑ / — — — / — / ⏑

12. **Bhmā sagayuttā Rummavatī sā.**

The metre which has a Bhagaṇa, a Magaṇa, a Sagaṇa and a Guru is called Rummavatī (Sk. Rukmavatī).

E.g.,

⏑ — —/⏑ ⏑ ⏑/— — ⏑/⏑ .

13. Ñeyyā Mattā mabhasagayuttā.

The metre which has a Magaṇa, a Bhagaṇa, a Sagaṇa and a Guru is known as Mattā.

E.g.,

⏑ ⏑ ⏑/⏑ — —/— — ⏑/⏑ .

14. Campakamālā ce bhamasā go.

If there are a Bhagana, a Magaṇa, a Sagaṇa and a Guru the metre is called Campakamālā.

E.g.,

⏑ — —/⏑ ⏑ ⏑/— — ⏑/⏑ .

N. B.—This is just the same as the Rummavatī given above. This must, therefore, be a mistake.

15. Narajagehi sā Manoramā.

The metre which contains a Nagaṇa, a Ragaṇa, a Jagaṇa and a Guru is called Manoramā.

E.g.,

— — —/⏑ — ⏑/— ⏑ —/⏑ .

16. Ubbhāsakantaṁ ce to marāl ca.

If there are a Tagaṇa, a Magaṇa, a Ragaṇa and a Laghu the metre is called Ubbhāsaka.

E.g.,

⏑ ⏑ —/⏑ ⏑ ⏑/⏑ — ⏑/—

(A metre corresponding to this is not found in the Vṛttaratnākara. The Sanskrit form of the name would be Udbhāṣaka).

Tuṭṭhubha (11 letters).

17. Tjā jgā garunāyamupaṭṭhitā sā.

The metre which has a Tagaṇa, and two Jagaṇas and also two Gurus is called Upaṭṭhitā (Sk. Upaṣṭhitā).

E.g.,

⏑ ⏑ — / — ⏑ — / — ⏑ — / ⏑ / ⏑ .

18. Indādikā tā vajirā jagā go.

If there are two Tagaṇas and a Jagaṇa and two Gurus the metre is called Indavajirā (Sk. Indravajrā).

E.g.,

⏑ ⏑ — / ⏑ ⏑ — / — ⏑ — / ⏑ / ⏑ .

19. Upādikā sāva jatā jagā go.

But the metre which has a Jagaṇa, a Tagaṇa, a Jagaṇa and two Gurus is called Upindavajirā (Sk. Upendravajrā).

E.g.,

— ⏑ — / ⏑ ⏑ — / — ⏑ — / ⏑ / ⏑

20. Anantarodīritalakkhaṇā ce.
Pādā vimissā Upajātayo tā ;
Evaṁ kiraññāsupi missitāsu,
Vadanti jātisvidameva nāma.

If the lines having the characteristics mentioned above are mixed in a verse it is called Upajāti. In the same way if other kinds of Vuttas are mixed in verses they are also known by the same name (*i.e.*, Upajāti).

In the above verse we find the first and the last lines are of Upindavajirā, and the second and the third lines are of Indavajirā. In the same way we may find instances where Vaṁsaṭṭha and Indravaṁsa, and Vasantatilakā and Indavajirā are mixed up.

21. Sajajā lagā gaditā Sumukhī.

If there are a Sagaṇa and two Jagaṇas and also a Laghu and a Guru the metre is called Sumukhī.

E.g.,

— — ⏑ / — ⏑ — / — ⏑ — / — / ⏑ .

N. B.—In the Vṛttaratnākara we find that it is "Najajalaga," that makes Sumukhi, thus substituting a Nagaṇa for the Sagaṇa of this book.

22. Dodhaka micchati ce bhabhabhā gā.

If there are three Bhagaṇas and two Gurus the metre is called Dodhaka.

E.g.,

⏑ — — / ⏑ — — / ⏑ — — / ⏑ / ⏑.

23. Vedassehi mtātagāg Sālini sā.

If there are a Magaṇa, two Tagaṇas and two Gurus, and if there is a pause after four and seven letters respectively the metre is called Sālinī (Sk. Śālinī).

E.g.,

⏑ / ⏑ ⏑ — / ⏑ ⏑ — / ⏑ / ⏑ .

Veda = 4; Assa = 7.

24. Vātummī sā yati Sāmbhā tagā go.

If there are a Magaṇa, a Bhagaṇa, a Tagaṇa and two Gurus and the same pause (as in the above) the metre is called Vātummī (Sk. Vātormī).

E.g.,

⌣ ⌣ ⌣ / ⌣ — — / ⌣ ⌣ — / ⌣ / ⌣ .

25. Bhā tanagā go sura Sasirī sā.

If after a Bhagaṇa there are Tagaṇa nagaṇas and two Gurus and if there is pause after five and six letters respectively the metre is called Sirī (Sk. Srī or Strī.) It is also called Māuktikamālā.

E.g.,

⌣ — — / ⌣ ⌣ — / — — — / ⌣ / ⌣ .

26. Ro narā idha Rathoddhatā lagā.

If there are a Ragaṇa, a Nagaṇa, a Ragaṇa, and also a Laghu and a Guru, the metre is called Rathoddhatā.

E.g.,

⌣ — ⌣ / — — — / ⌣ — ⌣ / — / ⌣ .

27. Svāgateti ranabhā gurukā dve.

If there are a Ragaṇa, a Nagaṇa, a Bhagaṇa and two Gurus the metre is called Svāgatā.

E.g.

⌣ — ⌣ / — — — / ⌣ — — / ⌣ / ⌣ .

28. Nanaralahugurūhi Bhaddikā.

By two Nagaṇas and a Ragaṇa and also a Laghu and a Guru we get Bhaddikā (Sk. Bhadrikā, Subhadrikā or Candrikā).

E.g.,

— — — / — — — / ⌣ — ⌣ / — / ⌣ .

Jagati (12 letters).

29. Vadanti Vaṁsaṭṭhamidaṁ jatā jarā.

When there are a Jagaṇa, a Tagaṇa, a Jagaṇa and a Ragaṇa the metre is called Vaṁsaṭṭha (Sk. Vaṁśastha).

— ⌣ — / ⌣ ⌣ — / — ⌣ — / ⌣ — ⌣ .

30. Sā Indavaṁsā khalu yattha tā jarā.

If there are two Tagaṇas and a Jagaṇa and a Ragaṇa the metre is called Indavaṁsā. (Sk. Indravaṁśā).

E.g.,

⌣ ⌣ — / ⌣ ⌣ — / — ⌣ — / ⌣ — ⌣ .

31. Idha toṭakamambudhisehi mitaṃ.

If a line is measured by four Sagaṇas (*i.e.*, if it contains four Sagaṇas) it is called Toṭaka.

E.g.,

— — ⌣ / — — ⌣ / — — ⌣ / — — ⌣ .

(Ambudhi = Samudda = 4.)

32. Dutavilambitamāha nabhā bharā.

When there are a Nagaṇa, two Bhagaṇas and a Ragaṇa the metre is called Dutavilambita (Sk. Drutavilambita.)

E.g.,

— — — / ⌣ — — / ⌣ — — / ⌣ — ⌣ .

33. Vasuyugaviratī nāmyā Puṭoyaṁ.

If in a line there is a pause after eight, and then after four letters, and if the line contains two Nagaṇas, a Magaṇa and a Yagaṇa, the metre is called Puṭa.

E.g.,

— — — / — — — / ⏑ ⏑ ⏑ / — ⏑ ⏑.

(Vasu=8. Yuga=4. Virati=Yati=Pause.)

34. Nayasahitā nyā Kusumavicittā.

If there are a Nagaṇa and a Yagaṇa joined with another Nagaṇa and a Yagaṇa the metre is called Kusumavicittā (Sk. Kusumavicitrā).

E.g.,

— — — / — ⏑ ⏑ / — — — / — ⏑ ⏑.

35. Bhujaṅgappayātaṁ bhave vedayehi.

If there are four Yagaṇas there will be Bhujaṅgappayāta (Sk. Bhujaṅgaprayāta.)

E.g.,

— ⏑ ⏑ / — ⏑ ⏑ / — ⏑ ⏑ / — ⏑ ⏑.

(Veda=4.)

36. Nabhajarehi bhavatip Piyaṁvadā.

If there are a Nagaṇa, a Bhagaṇa, a Jagaṇa and a Ragaṇa the metre is called Piyaṁvadā (Sk. Priyaṁvadā).

E.g.,

— — — / ⏑ — — / — ⏑ — / ⏑ — ⏑.

37. Vuttā sudhīhi Lalitā tabhā jarā.

If there are a Tagaṇa, a Bhagaṇa, a Jagaṇa and a Ragaṇa the metre is called Lalitā by the wise.

E.g.,

⏑ ⏑ — / ⏑ — — / — ⏑ — / ⏑ — ⏑ .

38. Pamitakkharā sajasasehuditā.

If there are a Sagaṇa and a Jagaṇa and again two Sagaṇas it is called Pamitakkharā (Sk. Pramitākṣarā).

E.g.,

— — ⏑ / — ⏑ — / — — ⏑ / — — ⏑ .

39. Nanabharasahitābhihitujjalā.

If there are two Nagaṇas and a Bhagaṇa and a Ragaṇa the metre is called Ujjalā (Sk. Ujvalā).

— — — / — — — / ⏑ — — / ⏑ — ⏑ .

40. Pancassacchinnā Vessadevī mamā yā.

If a line is divided by five and seven letters, and if it contains two Magaṇas and two Yagaṇas the metre is called Vessadevī (Sk. Vaisvadevī.)

E.g.,

⏑ ⏑ ⏑ / ⏑ ⏑ ⏑ / — ⏑ ⏑ / — ⏑ ⏑ .

(Assa=7.)

41. Vadatihi Tāmarasaṁ najajā yo.

If there are a Nagaṇa, two Jagaṇas and a Yagaṇa the metre is called Tāmarasa.

E.g.,

— — — / — ⏑ — / — ⏑ — / — ⏑ ⏑

42. Kamalāti ñeyyā sayasehi yo ve.

If there be a Yagaṇa after a Sagaṇa, a Yagaṇa and a Sagaṇa, it is called Kamalā.

E.g.,

— — ⌣ / — ⌣ ⌣ / — — ⌣ / — ⌣ ⌣ .

This is not to be found in the Vṛttaratnākara.

Atijagati (13 letters).

43. Mnā jrā go tidasayatippahāsinī sā.

If there are a Magaṇa, a Nagaṇa, a Jagaṇa, a Ragaṇa, and a Guru, and if there are pauses after three and ten letters, it is called Pahāsinī (Sk. Praharṣaṇī or Praharṣiṇī.)

E.g.,

⌣ ⌣ ⌣ / — — — / — ⌣ — / ⌣ — ⌣ / ⌣ .

44. Catuggahehiha Rucirā jabhā sajāg.

If there are pauses after four and nine letters, and if there are a Jagaṇa, a Bhagaṇa, a Sagaṇa, a Jagaṇa, and a Guru it is called Rucirā.

E.g..

— ⌣ — / ⌣ — — / — — ⌣ / — ⌣ — / ⌣ .

(Gaha = 9.)

Sakkarī (14 letters).

45. Nanarasalahugā sarehi' Parājitā.[1]

[1] Sarehaparajitā is better.

If there are two Nagaṇas and a Ragaṇa, a Sagaṇa, a Laghu and a Guru, and if there is a pause after seven letters, the metre is called Aparājitā.

E.g.,

— — — / — — — / ⏑ — ⏑ / — — ⏑ / — / ⏑.

(Sara = 7.)

46. Nanabhanalagitippaharaṇakalikā.

If there are two Nagaṇas, a Bhagaṇa, a Nagaṇa, a Laghu and a Guru, the metre is called Paharaṇakalikā (Sk. Praharaṇakalikā).

E.g.,

— — — / — — — / ⏑ — — / — — — / — / ⏑.

47. Vuttā Vasantatilakā tabhajā jagā go.

If there are a Tagaṇa, a Bhagaṇa, and two Jagaṇas and also two Gurus the metre is called Vasantatilakā.

E.g.,

⏑ ⏑ — / ⏑ — — / — ⏑ — / — ⏑ — / ⏑ / ⏑.

Atisakkarī (15 letters).

48. Dvihatahayalaghurathagiti Sasikalā.

If there are fourteen Laghus and a Guru the metre is called Sasikalā.

— — — — — — — — — — — — — — ⏑.

(Dvihata = multiplied by two. Haya = 7.)

49. Vasuhayayatiriha Maṇigaṇanikaro.

In the Sasikalā if there is a pause after eight and again after seven letters it is called Maṇigaṇanikara (Sk. Maṇiguṇanikara or Maṇigaṇakiraṇa).

E.g.,

— — — — — — — —, — — — — — — ⌣.

50. Nanamayayayutāyaṁ Mālinī bhogisīhi.

If there are two Nagaṇas, one Magaṇa and two Yagaṇas, and then pauses after eight and seven letters respectively the metre is called Mālinī.

E.g.,

— — — / — — — / ⌣ ⌣ ⌣ / — ⌣ ⌣ / — ⌣ ⌣.

(Bhogi=8. Isi=7.)

51. Bhavati najā bhajā rasahitā Pabhaddakaṁ.

If there are a Nagaṇa, a Jagaṇa, a Bhagaṇa, a Jagaṇa and a Ragaṇa the metre is called Pabhaddaka (Sk. Prabhadraka).

E.g.,

— — — / — ⌣ — / ⌣ — — / — ⌣ — / ⌣ — ⌣.

Aṭṭhi (16 letters).

52. Najabhajarā sadā bhavati Vāṇinī gayuttā.

If there are a Nagaṇa, a Jagaṇa, a Bhagaṇa, a Jagaṇa, and a Ragaṇa with a Guru the metre is called Vāṇinī.

E.g.,

— — — / — ⌣ — / ⌣ — — / — ⌣ — / ⌣ — ⌣ / ⌣.

N.B.—In a certain edition of the Vṛttaratnākara, in the place of Ragaṇa of this metre Tagaṇa is given. Then the line will stand as follows :—

— — — / — ⏑ — / ⏑ — — / — ⏑ — / ⏑ ⏑ — / / ⏑ .

Accaṭṭhi (17 letters).

53. Yamā no so bhalgā rasaharavirāmā Sikharinī.

If there are Ya, Ma, Na, Sa, Bha Gaṇas with a Laghu and a Guru, and if there are pauses after six and eleven letters the metre is called Sikhariṇī.

E.g.,

— ⏑ ⏑ / ⏑ ⏑ ⏑ /, — — — / — — ⏑ / ⏑ — — / — / ⏑ .

(Rasa=6. Hara=11.)

54. Rasayugisito no so mraslāg yadā Hariṇī tadā.

In a line if there are pauses after six, four and seven letters, and again, if there are Na, Sa, Ma, Ra, Sa Gaṇas with a Laghu and a Guru, the metre is called Hariṇī.

E.g.,

— — — / — — ⏑ / ⏑ ⏑ ⏑ / ⏑ — ⏑ / — — ⏑ / — / ⏑ .

55. Mandakkantā mabhanatatagā go yugutvassakehi.

If there are Ma, Bha, Na, Ta, Ta Gaṇas and two Gurus in a line, and if there are also pauses after four, six and seven lette rs the metre is called Mandakkantā (Sk. Mandākrāntā).

E.g.,

⏑ ⏑ ⏑ / ⏑ — — / — — — / ⏑ ⏑ — / ⏑ ⏑ — / ⏑ / ⏑ .

(Yuga=4. Utu=6. Assa=7.)

Dhuti (18 letters).

56. Mo to no yo yā Kusumitalatāvellitākkhutvisīhi.

If there are Magaṇa, Tagana, Nagaṇa, and three Yagaṇas and pauses after five, six and seven letters respectively the metre is called Kusumitalatāvellitā.

E.g.,

⏑ ⏑ ⏑ / ⏑ ⏑ — / — — — / — ⏑ ⏑ / — ⏑ ⏑ / — ⏑ ⏑.

(*Akkha*=5. Utu=6. Isi=7.)

Atidhuti [1] (19 letters).

57. Rasutvassehiymā nasararagurū Meghavipphūjitā sā.

If there are pauses after six, and again six and seven letters, and also Ya, Ma, Na, Sa, Ra, Ra Gaṇas and a Guru in a line, the metre is called Meghavipphūjitā (Sk. Meghavisphūrjitā).

E.g.,

— ⏑ ⏑ / ⏑ ⏑ ⏑ / — — — / — — ⏑ / ⏑ — ⏑ / ⏑ — ⏑ / ⏑.

58. Akkassehi Yadimsajā satatagā Saddūlavikkīḷitaṁ.

If there are pauses in a line after twelve and seven letters, and also Ma, Sa, Ja, Sa, Ta, Ta Gaṇas and a Guru, the metre is called Saddūlavikkīlita (Sk. Sārdūlavikrīḍita).

E.g.,

⏑ ⏑ ⏑ / — — ⏑ / — ⏑ — / — — ⏑ /, ⏑ ⏑ — / ⏑ ⏑ — / ⏑

(Akka=12.)

Kati (20 letters).

59. Vuttamīdisantu nāmato rajā rajā rajā gurū lahū ca.

[1] These terms may also stand in Pāli Dhiti and atidhiti.

If in a line Ragaṇa and Jagaṇa occur three times consecutively and then come a Guru and a Laghu the metre is called Vutta (Sk. Vṛtta).

E.g.,

⏑—⏑ / —⏑— / ⏑—⏑ / —⏑— / ⏑—⏑ / —⏑— / ⏑ / —.

Pakati (21 letters).

60. Mrabhnā yo yo trayenattimuniyatiyutā
Saddharā kittitāyaṁ.

If there are Ma, Ra, Bha, Na Gaṇas and three Yagaṇas and then pauses, one after every seventh letter, the metre is called Saddharā (Sk. Sragdharā).

E.g.,

⏑⏑⏑ / ⏑—⏑ / ⏑—— / ——— / —⏑⏑ / —⏑⏑ / —⏑⏑.

(Muni=7.)

Ākati (22 letters).

61. Bhrā naranāranātha ca guruddasakkaviramaṁ
hi Bhaddakamidaṁ.

If there are Bha, Ra, Na, Ra, Na, Ra, Na Gaṇas and a Guru and also pauses after ten and twelve letters, the metre is called Bhaddaka (Sk. Bhadraka or Prabhadraka).

E.g.,

⏑ — — / ⏑ — ⏑ / — — — / ⏑ — ⏑ / — — — /

⏑ — ⏑ / — — — / ⏑.

Iti Vuttodaye Samavuttaparicchedo tatiyo.

Thus ends the third Chapter of the Vuttodaya which deals with the regular metres.

CATUTTHO PARICCHEDO.

FOURTH CHAPTER.

1. Visame yadi sā salagā same,
Bhattayato gurukā Upacittaṁ.

If there are three Sagaṇas and a Laghu and a Guru in the odd lines, and three Bhagaṇas followed by two Gurus in the even lines, the metre is called Upacitta (Sk. Upacitra).

E.g.,

— — ⏑ / — — ⏑ / — — ⏑ / — / ⏑,
⏑ — — / ⏑ — — / ⏑ — — / ⏑ / ⏑.

2. Bhattayato yadi gā Dutamajjhā
Yadi punareva bhavanti najājyā.

If there are two Gurus after three Bhagaṇas (in the odd lines), and one Nagaṇa, two Jagaṇas and a Yagaṇa (in the even lines), the metre is called Dutamajjhā (Sk. Drutamadhyā).

E.g.,

⏑ — — / ⏑ — — / ⏑ — — / ⏑ / ⏑,
— — — / — ⏑ — / — ⏑ — / — ⏑ ⏑.

3. Yadi sattitayaṁ guruyuttaṁ,
Vegavatī yadi bhattitayā gā.

If there are three Sagaṇas with a Guṛu (in the odd lines) and three Bhagaṇas and two Gurus (in the even lines) the metre is called Vegavatī.

E.g.,

— — ⌣ / — — ⌣ / — — ⌣ / ⌣,

⌣ — — / ⌣ — — / ⌣ — — / ⌣ / ⌣.

4. To jo visame rato Gurū ca,
Msā jgā Bhaddavirājamettha go ce.

If there are Ta, Ja, Ra Gaṇas and a Guru in the odd lines, and Ma, Sa, Ja Gaṇas and two Gurus in the even lines, the metre is called Bhaddavirāja (Sk. Bhadravirad).

E.g.,

⌣ ⌣ — / — ⌣ — / ⌣ — ⌣ / ⌣,

⌣ ⌣ ⌣ / — — ⌣ / ⌣ ⌣ — / ⌣ / ⌣.

5. Visame sajā saguruyuttā.
Ketumatī same bharanagā go.

If there are Sa, Ja, Sa Gaṇas and a Guru in the odd lines, and Bha, Ra, Na Gaṇas and two Gurus in the even lines, the metre is called Ketumatī.

E.g.,

— — ⌣ / — ⌣ — / — — ⌣ / ⌣,

⌣ — — / ⌣ — ⌣ / — — — / ⌣ / ⌣.

6. Akhyātikā tā visame jagā go,
Jatā jagā go tu same'tha pāde.

If there are two Tagaṇas, one Jagaṇa, and two Gurus in the odd lines, and a Jagaṇa, a Tagaṇa, and a Jagaṇa and two Gurus in the even lines, the metre is called Akyātikā.
(Some read as Akhyānikā (Sk. Akhyātakī or Akhyānakī).

E.g.,

⌣ ⌣ — / ⌣ ⌣ — / — ⌣ — / ⌣ / ⌣,

— ⌣ — / ⌣ ⌣ — / — ⌣ — / ⌣ / ⌣.

7. Jatā jagā go visame same tu,
Tā jo gagā ce viparītapubbā.

If there are Ja, Ta, Ja Gaṇas and two Gurus in the odd lines, and two Tagaṇas, one Jagaṇa and two Gurus in the even lines the metre is called Viparītākhyātikā.

(Or Viparītākhyānikā. See above.)

E.g.,

— ⏑ — / ⏑ ⏑ — / — ⏑ — / ⏑ / ⏑,

⏑ ⏑ — / ⏑ ⏑ — / — ⏑ — / ⏑ / ⏑.

8. Sasato salagā visame same,
Nabhabharā bhavati Hariṇaplutā.

If there are three Sagaṇas and a Laghu and a Guru in the odd lines, and one Nagaṇa, two Bhagaṇas and a Ragaṇa in the even lines, the metre is called Hariṇaplutā.

E.g.,

— — ⏑ / — — ⏑ / — — ⏑ / — / ⏑,

— — — / ⏑ — — / ⏑ — — / ⏑ — ⏑.

9. Yadi nanaralagā najā jarā,
Yadi ca tadā'paravattamicchati.

If there are two Nagaṇas, one Ragaṇa and a Laghu and a Guru (in the odd lines), and one Nagaṇa, two Jagaṇas, and one Ragaṇa (in the even lines), the metre is called Aparavatta (Sk Aparavaktra).

E.g.,

— — — / — — — / ⏑ — ⏑ / — / ⏑,

— — — / — ⏑ — / — ⏑ — / ⏑ — ⏑.

10. Visamamupagatā nanā rayā ce,
Najajaragā samake ca Pupphitaggā.

If there are two Nagaṇas, one Ragaṇa and one Yagaṇa in the odd lines, and one Nagaṇa, two Jagaṇas, one Ragaṇa and a Guru in the even lines the metre is called Pupphitaggā (Sk. Puṣpitāgrā).

E.g.,

— — — / — — — / ⏑ — ⏑ / — ⏑ ⏑,
— — — / — ⏑ — / — ⏑ — / ⏑ — ⏑ / ⏑.

11. Sā yavādikā matī rajā rajā tu,
Same'same jarā jarā gurū bhaveyyuṁ.

If there are two sets of Ragaṇa-Jagaṇas in the odd lines and again two sets of Jagaṇa-Ragaṇas and a Guru in the even lines, the metre is called Yavamatī.

E.g.,

⏑ — ⏑ / — ⏑ — / ⏑ — ⏑ / — ⏑ —,
— ⏑ — / ⏑ — ⏑ / — ⏑ — / ⏑ — ⏑ ⏑.

Iti Addhasamavutta paricchedo catuttho.

Thus ends the fourth Chapter which deals with metres that are partly regular.

PAÑCAMO PARICCHEDO.

[1] FIFTH CHAPTER.

1. Naṭṭhakkharesu pādesu,
   Snādimhā yoṇṇavā Vattaṁ

In a line of eight letters if there is neither a Sagaṇa nor a Nagaṇa after the first letter, but there is a Yagaṇa after the first four letters, the metre is called Vatta (Sk. Vaktra).

E.g., Ya

⏑ ⏑ — ⏑ / — ⏑ ⏑ / —,

⏑ ⏑ ⏑ ⏑ / — ⏑ ⏑ / ⏑.

2. Samesu sindhuto jena
   Pathyāvattaṁ pakittitaṁ.

In even lines if there is a Jagaṇa **after the first four** letters (all others being like the **preceding one) the metre is** called Pathyāvatta (Sk. Pathyāvaktra).

E.g.,

— ⏑ — ⏑ / — ⏑ ⏑ / —,

Ja

⏑ ⏑ ⏑ ⏑ / — ⏑ — / ⏑.

3. Ojesu jena sindhuto,
   Tameva viparītādi.

If there is a Jagaṇa in odd lines (after the first four letters) the metre is called Viparītapathyāvatta.

[1] This chapter is placed among those of Mattāvuttas in the Vṛttaratnākara. It is to be found there just before Mātrasamaka and has been called Anustupprakaraṇa or Vaktraprakaraṇa.

E.g., Ja

⏑ ⏑ — ⏑ / — ⏑ — / ⏑,

— ⏑ — — / — ⏑ ⏑ / —

4. Nakāro ce jaladhito,
   Capalāvattamiccetaṁ.

If there is a Nagaṇa (after the first four letters in the odd lines) it is called Capalāvatta (Sk. Capalāvaktra).

E.g., Na

— ⏑ ⏑ ⏑ / — — — / ⏑,

— — ⏑ ⏑ / — ⏑ ⏑ / ⏑.

5. Same lo sattame yassā,
   Vipulā Piṅgalassa sā.

If in the even lines of the above metre the seventh letter is a Laghu it is the Vipulā of Piṅgala.

E.g.,

— ⏑ ⏑ ⏑ / — ⏑ ⏑ / ⏑,

L

— — ⏑ ⏑ — ⏑ / — / — / ⏑.

N.B.—These sets of lines must be doubled to get complete verses.

6. Setavassākhilesupi.

In the opinion of Setava (Sk. Saitava) there should be a Laghu in the seventh place in all the four lines in order that the metre be called a Vipulā.

7. Bhenaṇṇavā tabbipulā.

If there is a Bhagaṇa after the first four letters in each line the metre is called Bhavipulā.

E.g., Bha

⏑ ⏑ — ⏑ / ⏑ — — / ⏑.

8. Evamaññā ro catutthā.

The other one in which there is a Ragaṇa after the first four letters is also thus named (*i.e.*, Ravipulā).

E.g., Ra

⏑ — ⏑ ⏑ / ⏑ — ⏑ / ⏑.

9. No'ṇṇavā Navipulā.

If after the first four letters there is a Nagaṇa the metre is called Navipulā.

E.g., Na

⏑ — ⏑ ⏑ / — — — / ⏑.

10. To'ṇṇavā tathā'ññā siyā.

Another one in which there is a Tagaṇa after the first four letters is named as such (*i.e.*, Tavipulā).

E.g., Ta

⏑ — ⏑ — / ⏑ ⏑ — / ⏑.

N.B.—All these lines must be quadrupled to make complete verses.

11. Nadissatettha yaṁ chandaṁ,
Payoge dissate yadi,
Visamakkharapādantaṁ,
Gāthā sāmaññanāmato.

If there is any Chanda (*i.e.*, a metre—and therefore a verse of a particular metre) that is not seen here, but seen in usage, it, having lines of irregular letters, is called by the general name of Gāthā.

Iti Visamavuttaparicchedo pañcamo.

Thus ends the fifth Chapter dealing with irregular metres.

CHAṬṬHO PARICCHEDO

SIXTH CHAPTER.

Patthāravidhi.

The method of Tabulation.

1. Patthāre sabbage pāde,
Pubbagādholpare samā,
Pubbegurutvevamime,
Kattabbā yāva sabbalo.

In Patthāra (*i.e.*, Tabulation), under the first Guru of the line consisting of Gurus only, there should be a Laghu. After it, all must be the same as above. Before it there should be only Gurus. This should be repeated till the line consisting of Laghus only is arrived at.

Explanation.

Patthāra is the method by which the different Vuttas of a Chanda is found out. This is something like permutation and combination in Algebra. This is done in the following way:

1. First of all write down the line that contains Gurus only.

2. Then write a Laghu under the first Guru.

It is to be noted that the first Guru, though it occupies the first place in the first line, may occupy any other place in other lines.

3. The spaces (if any) on the right hand side of the Laghu, should always be filled up with Laghus and Gurus

just according as those in the corresponding spaces of the preceding line.

4. But the spaces (if any) on the left hand side of the Laghu must be filled up with Gurus only irrespective of what the corresponding spaces in the above line contain.

5. Continue in this way till the line which contains only Laghus is arrived at.

For example :

Take the line that contains Gurus only of the Chanda called Suppatiṭṭhā (*i.e.*, the Chanda of five letters). It will stand as ⌣ ⌣ ⌣ ⌣ ⌣.

Now, write down a Laghu under the first Guru of this line, and fill up the remaining four places with Gurus, because there are Gurus only in the corresponding places of the above line. It will then stand as — ⌣ ⌣ ⌣ ⌣ .

Again write a Laghu under the first Guru of this line. (Now the first Guru of this line occupies the second place of the line.) Fill up the right hand side of this with three Gurus as above. But the space on the left hand side must be filled up with a Guru irrespective of the Laghu that occupies the corresponding place in the preceding line. It will then stand as ⌣ — ⌣ ⌣ ⌣ .

The fourth line, similarly, will be — — ⌣ ⌣ ⌣ . Here the first Laghu occupies the place under the first Guru of the above line. The second Laghu is written to correspond with the Laghu in the same place of the line above. The three Gurus that come after these Laghus have been written down in accordance with those in the above line.

The fifth line would be ⌣ ⌣ — ⌣ ⌣ . Here the Laghu that occupies the third place is the one written under the first Guru of the fourth line, and the two Gurus on the right hand side of it are written down corresponding to the two Gurus in the above line. The two Gurus on the left hand side of it are those that are written to fill up the remaining spaces irrespective of what the preceding line contains.

The complete Patthāra of this Chanda (Suppatiṭṭhā) and also that of four letters (*i.e.*, Patiṭṭhā) is given below.

Patiṭṭhā	Suppatiṭṭhā
⏑ ⏑ ⏑ ⏑	⏑ ⏑ ⏑ ⏑ ⏑
	— ⏑ ⏑ ⏑ ⏑
— ⏑ ⏑ ⏑	⏑ — ⏑ ⏑ ⏑
	— — ⏑ ⏑ ⏑
⏑ — ⏑ ⏑	⏑ ⏑ — ⏑ ⏑
	— ⏑ — ⏑ ⏑
— — ⏑ ⏑	⏑ — — ⏑ ⏑
	— — — ⏑ ⏑
⏑ ⏑ — ⏑	⏑ ⏑ ⏑ — ⏑
	— ⏑ ⏑ — ⏑
— ⏑ — ⏑	⏑ — ⏑ — ⏑
	— — ⏑ — ⏑
⏑ — — ⏑	⏑ ⏑ — — ⏑
	— ⏑ — — ⏑
— — — ⏑	⏑ — — — ⏑
	— — — — ⏑
⏑ ⏑ ⏑ —	⏑ ⏑ ⏑ ⏑ —
	— ⏑ ⏑ ⏑ —
— ⏑ ⏑ —	⏑ — ⏑ ⏑ —
	— — ⏑ ⏑ —
⏑ — ⏑ —	⏑ ⏑ — ⏑ —
	— ⏑ — ⏑ —
— — ⏑ —	⏑ — — ⏑ —
	— — — ⏑ —
⏑ ⏑ — —	⏑ ⏑ ⏑ — —
	— ⏑ ⏑ — —
— ⏑ — —	⏑ — ⏑ — —
	— — ⏑ — —
⏑ — — —	⏑ ⏑ — — —
	— ⏑ — — —
— — — —	⏑ — — — —
	— — — — —

Points to be remembered :—

1. First of all write the line that contains Gurus only.

2. Write a Laghu always under the first Guru.

3. The right hand side of the Laghu should be filled up with the Gurus or the Laghus as the preceding line.

4. The left hand side of the Laghu should be filled up only with Gurus.

5. Repeat this till the line containing Laghus only is arrived at. In the Patthāra of Patiṭṭhā which is a Chanda of four letters given above the first line is the Vutta which has only Gurus. Then writing a Laghu under the first Guru we get the line which contains a Laghu at the beginning and then three Gurus. Then by writing a Laghu under the first Guru of that line, which is of course the second letter of the line we get the third line having a Guru at the beginning and then a Laghu and following it two Gurus. Here the first Guru has come according to the rule that the left hand side should be filled up by only Gurus. Then in the fourth line we have two Laghus at the beginning and then two Gurus. Here the first Laghu we get according to the rule of writing a Laghu under the first Guru of the preceding line, and the second Laghu comes according to the rule of filling up the right hand side in accordance with the Gurus or Laghus that the preceding line contains. Thus all the succeeding lines should be traced till we come to the line which does not contain any more Guru under which to write a Laghu.

Iti Patthāravidhi.

Thus ends the method of Tabulation.

Natthavidhi.

The method of finding out the arrangement of Gurus and Laghus of a particular Vutta in a given Chanda.

2. Naṭṭhassa yo bhaveyyaṅko, tasmiṁ loddhīkate same ;
Visame tvekasahite, Bhaveyyaddhīkate guru.

When the serial number of the lost Vutta is divided by two, write a Laghu in case if the dividend is an even number ; and if the number is an odd one add one to it and divide it by two and write a Guru.

Explanation.

Naṭṭha means that which is lost or unknown. Therefore Naṭṭhavidhi means the method by which we find out the arrangement of Gurus and Laghus in a given Vutta of a given Chanda.

The method followed in this case is to divide the serial number of the Vutta by two and to write a Laghu if the dividend is an even number, and a Guru if it is an odd number, and to repeat this till the number of letters that the particular Chanda contains is obtained, adding one in every case when the quotient is an odd number so that it may be divided by two without leaving a remainder.

For instance, if any one wants to know what will be the form of the sixth Vutta of the Chanda of five letters, *i.e.*, Suppatiṭṭhā, he should proceed thus :—

1. The serial number of the Vutta of which we want to know the form is 6 ; therefore write 6.

2. Divide this by 2.

3. Now, as the dividend is an even number write a Laghu.

4. Our quotient is 3.

5. This is an odd number and therefore cannot be divided by 2 without leaving a remainder. So add 1 to it and divide by 2. But as our original dividend here is an odd number write a Guru. Thus we get a Laghu and a Guru as the first and the second letters of the Vutta.

6. Now, our quotient is 2. Divide this by 2, and write a Laghu.

7. Then the quotient is 1 ; add 1 to this and divide by 2, and write a Guru. The next step will be the same as this. Thus we have come to the 5th letter. Now we should stop,

because the Chanda to which the Vutta belongs contains only five letters.

Thus the Vutta we want will stand as, — ⏑ — ⏑ ⏑.
We can test the correctness of this result by comparing it with the table in p. 46.

Iti Naṭṭhavidhi.

Thus ends the method of finding out the lost metre.

Udditthavidhi.

The method of finding out the place of a Vutta in the Patthāra of its Chanda.

3. Ekādinukkamenaṅke, pubbādho diguṇe likhe;
Missitehi lahuṭṭhehi, sekehudditthakambhave.

Numbers from one multiplied by two successively should be written in order in all the places of the letters from the beginning to the end of the given line. Then, the sum of the numbers that stand in the places of Laghus increased by one is the Uddiṭṭhaka (or the serial number of the given Vutta in the table of the Patthāra of its Chanda).

Uddiṭṭha means that which is meant or given. Uddiṭṭhavidhi, therefore, means the method of finding out the place that a given Vutta occupies in the tabulation of its Chanda.

The procedure in this case is as follows :—

First write the Gurus and Laghus of the Vutta in a line. Then write 1 above the first letter. Next write the double of 1, *i.e.*, 2, over the next letter. Then write the double of 2, *i.e.*, 4, over the third letter. In this way go on till the last letter of the line. Then add together all the numbers that stand over the Laghus. To this sum, again, add 1. This is the number which indicates the place of the Vutta in the tabulation of its Chanda.

For instance, let ⏑ — — ⏑ — be the Vutta given. Now, to find out its place in the Tabulation (Patthāra) of its Chanda proceed thus:—First write 1 above the first letter, then 2 above the second, then 4 above the third, and 8 above the fourth and then 16 above the fifth, thus multiplying the numbers by 2 in each time. Then find out the numbers that stand above the Laghus. They are 2, 4, and 16 in this case. Now, add them together. Then the sum would be 22. To this sum add 1 more. The result is 23. So the Vutta is the 23rd in the table. (By comparing this with the table on p. 46 the correctness of this can be tested).

Iti Udditthavidhi.

[Thus ends the method of finding out the place of a given Vutta in the Patthāra of its Chanda.

Lagakriyavidhi.

The method of finding out the number of Vuttas of different type in a given Chanda.

4. Vuttakkharasamā sankhyā, likhya sekoparūpari,
Ekekahīnamekādi, nuṭṭhāne sabbagādikaṁ.

One above another, write as many units as there are letters in the Chanda with one unit more. Then, by adding together these (one to the other) leaving only the last one, we get the number of Vuttas such as Sabba-Guru Vutta, etc., in a particular Chanda.

Lagakriyā is the method by which the number of Vuttas of different forms in a Chanda is found out.

If any one wants to know how many Vuttas there are in a particular Chanda and how many of them are Sabba-laghu, and how many are Sabba-guru and so on, he should proceed thus :—

First let him write as many units as there are letters in the given Vutta one above the other, and then one more unit.

Vuttasankhyāvidhi.

The method of finding out the total number of Vuttas in a given Chanda.

5. [1]Lagakriyāṅkasandohe—bhave saṅkyā vimissite,
Uddiṭṭhaṅkasamāhāro—seko ve maṁ saṃānaye.

The total number (of the Vuttas of a Chanda) will be (what is got) by adding the numbers that are in Lagakriyā.[1] Or the sum of the numbers in Uddiṭṭha with one more will also give this number.

The above is the method by which we can get the total number of Vuttas in a given Chanda.

If we want to know what is the total number of a particular Chanda we can get it either by adding the numbers in Lagakriyā, or by adding the numbers in the Uddiṭṭha and increasing it by one.

For instance, the numbers that we got above in the Lagakriyā of the Chanda of five letters is, from top to bottom, 1,5,10,10,5,1. Now, their sum is 32. Then this is the number of Vuttas that the particular Chanda contains.

Again, in the Uddiṭṭha of the same Chanda we had 1,2,4, 8,16. Now, their sum is 31. When we add 1 to this sum it will be 32. This is just the same as the above.

Iti Vuttasaṅkhyāvidhi.

Thus ends the method of finding out the number of Vuttas in a Chanda.

Pattharabhūmimānavidhi.

The method of finding out the space that will be occupied by the Patthāra of a Chanda.

[1] In the Vuttodaya and in its Tikā the term Gurukriyā is used for the term Lagakriyā. But the term Lagakriyā is the one generally used and the more appropriate

6. Saṅkhyeva dviguṇekūna—Vitthārāyāmasambhavo,
Vuttassaddhantarānañca—garulānañca aṅgulaṁ.

[1]The space occupied by a Chanda is the same as the number of Vuttas of it multiplied by two and minus one in inches. There should be one inch between (each two lines) and between each two Gurus or Laghus (*i.e.*, between two letters).

Iti Patthārabhūmimānavidhi.

Thus ends the method of measuring the space that is required for writing down a Patthāra.

Iti [2] *Chappaccayavibhāgo nāma chaṭṭho paricchedo.*

Thus ends the sixth Chapter dealing with Chappaccaya.

Iti Saṅgharakkhitattherapādaviracitaṁ Vuttodayaṁ Niṭṭhitaṁ.

Thus ends the Vuttodaya composed by the Venerable Saṇgharakhita Thera.

[1] In ancient days it was the custom in India to write down those things either on sands or on the specially prepared ground. Hence the mention of inches.

[2] Patthāro naṭṭhamuddiṭṭhamekadvādilagakriyā,
Saṅkhyānamaddhayogo ca—chaḷete paccayā matā.

Tikā.